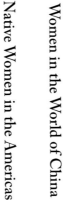

WOMEN'S ISSUES:
GLOBAL TRENDS

WOMEN IN THE WORLD OF RUSSIA

BY
AUTUMN LIBAL

Mason Crest Publishers
Philadelphia

The author would like to thank Olga Bochkaryova for her invaluable insights and helpful commentary.

Mason Crest Publishers Inc.
370 Reed Road
Broomall, Pennsylvania 19008
(866) MCP-BOOK (toll free)
www.masoncrest.com

13 12 11 10 09 08 07 06   10 9 8 7 6 5 4 3 2

Library of Congress Cataloging-in-Publication Data

Libal, Autumn.
Women in the world of Russia / by Autumn Libal.
    p. cm. — (Women's issues, global trends)
Includes bibliographical references and index.
ISBN 1-59084-866-7   ISBN 1-59084-856-X (series)
1. Women—Russia (Federation)—Juvenile literature. 2. Women—Russia—History—Juvenile literature. I. Title. II. Series.
HQ1665.15.L53 2005
305.4'0947—dc22

                                                   200400758 8

Interior design by Michelle Bouch and MK Bassett-Harvey.
Illustrations by Michelle Bouch.
Produced by Harding House Publishing Service, Inc.
www.hardinghousepages.com
Cover design by Benjamin Stewart.
Printed in India.

CONTENTS

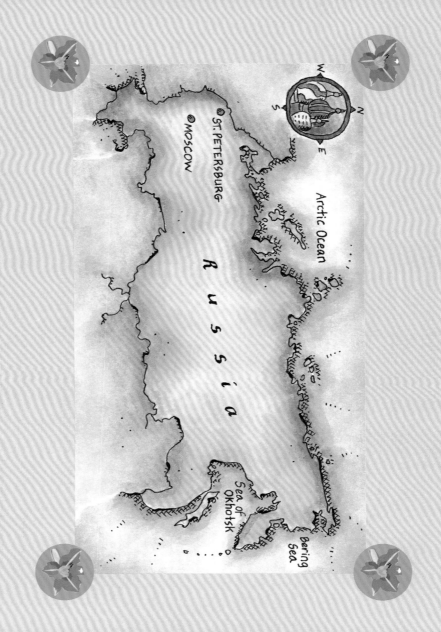

INTRODUCTION

by Mary Jo Dudley

The last thirty years have been a time of great progress for women around the world. In some countries, especially where women have more access to education and work opportunities, the relationships between women and men have changed radically. The boundaries between men's roles and women's roles have been crossed, and women are enjoying many experiences that were denied them in past centuries.

But there is still much to be done. On the global stage, women are increasingly the ones who suffer most from poverty. At the same time that they produce 75 to 90 percent of the world's food crops, they are also responsible for taking care of their households. According to the United Nations, in no country in the world do men come anywhere near to spending as much time on housework as women do. This means that women's job opportunities are often extremely limited, contributing to the "feminization of poverty."

In fact, two out of every three poor adults are women. According to the Decade of Women, "Women do two-thirds of the world's work, receive 10 percent of the world's income, and own one percent of the means of production." Women often have no choice but to take jobs that lack long-term security or adequate pay; many women work in dangerous working conditions or in unprotected home-based industries. This series clearly illustrates how historic events and contemporary trends (such as war, conflicts, and migration) have also contributed to women's loss of property and diminished access to resources.

A recent report from Human Rights Watch indicates that many countries continue to deny women basic legal protections. Amnesty International points out, "Governments are not living up to their promises under the Women's Convention to protect women from discrimination and violence such as rape and female genital mutilation." Many nations—including the United States—have not ratified the United Nations' Women's Treaty.

During times of armed conflict, especially under policies of ethnic cleansing, women are particularly at risk. Murder, torture, systematic rape, forced pregnancy, and forced abortions are all too common human rights violations endured by women around the world. This series presents the experience of women in Vietnam, Cambodia, the Middle East, and other war-torn regions.

In the political arena, equality between men and women has still not been achieved. Around the world, women are underrepresented in their local and national governments; on average, women represent only 10 percent of all legislators worldwide. This series provides excellent examples of key female leaders who have promoted women's rights and occupied unique leadership positions, despite historical contexts that would normally have shut them out from political and social prominence.

The Fourth World Conference on Women called upon the international community to take action in the following areas of concern:

- the persistent and increasing burden of poverty on women
- inequalities and inadequacies in access to education and training
- inequalities and inadequacies in access to health care and related services
- violence against women

- the effects of armed or other kinds of conflict on women
- inequality in economic structures and policies, in all forms of productive processes, and in access to resources
- insufficient mechanisms at all levels to promote the advancement of women
- lack of protection of women's human rights
- stereotyping of women and inequality in women's participation in all community systems, especially the media
- gender inequalities in the management of natural resources and the safeguarding of the environment
- persistent discrimination against and violation of the rights of female children

The Conference's mission statement includes these sentences: "Equality between women and men is a matter of human rights and a condition for social justice and is also a necessary and fundamental prerequisite for equality, development and peace . . . equality between women and men is a condition . . . for society to meet the challenges of the twenty-first century." This series provides examples of how women have risen above adversity, despite their disadvantaged social, economic, and political positions.

Each book in WOMEN'S ISSUES: GLOBAL TRENDS takes a look at women's lives in a different key region or culture, revealing the history, contributions, triumphs, and challenges of women around the world. Women play key roles in shaping families, spirituality, and societies. By interweaving historic backdrops with the modern-day evolving role of women in the home and in society at large, this series presents the important part women play as cultural communicators. Protection of women's rights is an integral part of universal human rights, peace, and economic security. As a result, readers who gain understanding of women's lives around the world will have deeper insight into the current condition of global interactions.

"THEY TALK ABOUT A WOMAN'S SPHERE, AS THOUGH IT HAD A LIMIT. THERE'S NOT A PLACE IN EARTH OR HEAVEN, THERE'S NOT A TASK TO MANKIND GIVEN . . . WITHOUT A WOMAN IN IT."
—KATE FIELD

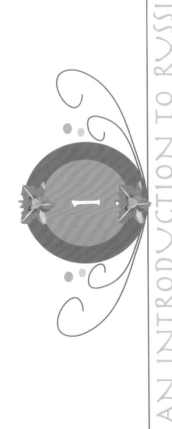

AN INTRODUCTION TO RUSSIA

1

In all parts of the world, women play key roles in their societies. Women participate in the social structures of communities, the governments of states, and the development of *economies*. Russia is no exception, and we can't understand Russian society without understanding the lives of Russian women and the important contributions they make.

Russia's sheer size makes it home to diverse geographies, climates, and peoples. Women's roles vary across regions and have changed much throughout history. In order to best understand the lives of women in Russia today, we must first have a general understanding of the region and some of the major historical events that have influenced Russian people's lives.

Russia, the largest nation on earth, is a vast country stretching from the Baltic Sea in the west to the Pacific Ocean in the east. The Arctic Ocean forms Russia's northern border. In the west and south, Russia borders numerous countries, including Finland, Ukraine, Kazakhstan, Mongolia, and Russia's largest neighbor, China.

Russia is an ancient land, deeply rooted in the past.

The Ural Mountains divide the country into two main regions. West of the Ural Mountains is considered part of Europe, while east of these mountains is considered part of Asia. Because of this division, many people refer to Russia's part of the world as Eurasia. Two-thirds of Russia is covered by forests, but the country also contains an arctic zone, frozen *tundra*, fertile farmlands, and even a very small subtropical zone near the Black Sea.

Russia's geographic and political boundaries are not the same today as they were years ago. This huge country's borders have shifted many times throughout history. In fact, it wasn't until the ninth century that a Russian state existed at all, and that state and its people would go through many transformations on their way to becoming what we think of as Russia today.

For thousands of years before the rise of the first Russian state, Eurasia was inhabited by many different groups of people. Some parts of Eurasia, especially the northeast, have very harsh climates and are not suitable for most types of agriculture. In these areas, people hunted, fished, and raised reindeer to support themselves and lived a *transient* way of life. This region was very isolated from other peoples and civilizations, so most people continued this lifestyle virtually uninterrupted. In the far reaches of Siberia, some people even continue living this way today.

West of the Ural Mountains, life was much different. Many of the important events leading up to the creation of a Russian state occurred in western Eurasia in the area lying between the Baltic and the Black Seas. The northern section of this region is forest, but the southern portion is well-suited to farming. This fertile land is called the steppe, and it stretches from what is present-day Ukraine to beyond the Ural Mountains.

The steppe is similar to the prairies of North America. Here, people adopted agricultural practices. However, instead of settling in permanent villages as

Horses were first domesticated on the steppe. The use of horses allowed people to be far more mobile and revolutionized warfare. Horse-borne armies caused much instability as wave after wave of invaders swept across the region. Furthermore, the domestication of horses had a huge influence, not only on the steppe, but on the history of the world.

many agriculturalists do, these communities moved frequently, sometimes staying in one place only long enough for crops to grow. Strong nomadic groups drove weaker populations from one place to another, and invasions were common. For this reason, many regional groups chose to live as hunter/gatherers in the forest rather than face the risks of agricultural life on the steppe.

For the two thousand years leading up to the *Common Era*, life west of the Ural Mountains underwent drastic changes. In these centuries, new technologies like metalworking and resources like furs and *amber* stimulated trade with Europe and Asia. Amber was especially valued and its trade steadily increased the amount of wealth in the region. Eventually, increased wealth concentrated in the hands of a few would lead to the rise of an *aristocracy*, forever altering life in Russia.

The complicated mix of increasing trade, wealth, and warfare continued in western Eurasia for hundreds of years. Then between 600 and 800 C.E., a combination of population growth and large migrations into the region caused new changes. Many ethnic groups, including Finns, Greeks, steppe nomads, Jews, and Slavs lived in the area. The Slavic population increased dramatically and became the dominant group. At the same time, the Scandinavians (also known as Norse or Vikings) moved in from the north. Interaction between the Slavs and the Norse began a whole new era in western Eurasia.

The eastern Slavs controlled the area from the city of Kiev in the South to Novgorod in the north. Trade developed along the area's various rivers. The Slavs in the north were often under attack from the Norse, who had to pass through the area to reach Constantinople, a wealthy city important for trade. Constantinople was also the center of *Orthodox* Christianity which would eventually become the dominant religion in Eastern Europe.

Economic troubles from trade interruptions and food shortages caused internal violence in the region. According to local history, in the ninth century C.E., the Slavic groups living in the forest zone near the Baltic Sea wanted

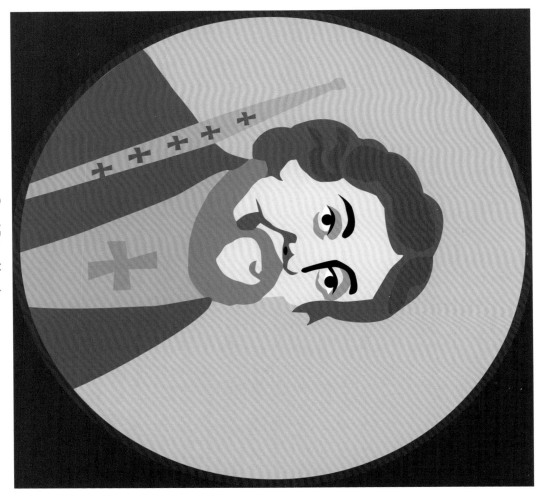

Grand Prince Yaroslav

greater unity among their peoples but could find no local leader strong enough to establish order. Then Prince Rurik, a strong Norse leader, landed on the Baltic shores and established rule over the local populations around Novgorod. The area became known as Rus, and Rurik made himself grand prince. Rurik, and later his son Oleg, steadily expanded this federation, eventually reaching Kiev and making it the capital. Rus was now a state, meaning it had defined boundaries and a central administration in the capital.

In Rus, a centralized government encouraged the further development of a *class hierarchy*. All the areas under state control had to pay *tribute* to the grand prince in Kiev. The lesser princes of the surrounding areas collected taxes from the peasant class. A portion of these taxes became the grand prince's tribute while the rest went to the local leaders. Tribute was given in the form of goods like furs, crops, and honey. Much of the tribute was then taken to Constantinople where it was sold. Under some princes, the tributes were manageable for the population, but under other princes the tributes could be extremely harsh.

Kiev flourished into the eleventh century. Tributes and trade made the ruling classes in Rus quite wealthy. Orthodox Christianity was adopted as the official religion of the state and would eventually become the Russian Orthodox Church. Orthodox missionaries created the cyrillic alphabet to give the Slavic people a written language with which to learn the Bible. Under the rule of Grand Prince Yaroslav (1036–1054 C.E.), the city became a major European center with eighty thousand people. This was approximately the same size as Paris and marked the height of the Kievan state.

In the twelfth century, Kievan Rus descended into disarray. Trade faltered, invasions into the steppe increased, and princes bickered among themselves for supremacy. Successive grand princes steadily lost control over the principalities, and in 1169 Kiev fell to an invasion by a lesser prince. The Kievan state had officially ceased to exist, and a new capital was established near the town of Moscow.

In 1237, the Tatar army, led by Batu Khan ushered in a new era for Russia. The Tatars, sometimes called the Mongols, invaded on horseback and massacred many of the inhabitants of Kiev and the surrounding area. Genghis Khan, Batu Khan's grandfather, had previously conquered much of China and Central Asia, and the Tatars now had a great empire. They would rule Russia for more than two hundred years, cutting off the region's contact with Western Europe and allowing Russian princes to collect taxes and rule only in the name of the Khan. The cultural development contact with Western Europe had all but ceased in Russia. Furthermore, the huge tributes demanded by the Khan were nearly impossible for the people to produce. Huge numbers of peasants fell into debt and were enslaved as *serfs*.

In 1327, the Tatar government gave Prince Ivan I of Moscow permission to collect taxes, not only from his own city, but from much of Tatar-controlled Russia. This led to an increase in the power of Moscow, and soon it became the capital city.

Eventually, the Russian princes would rebel against the Tatar Empire. In 1480, Ivan III, also known as Ivan the Great, finally defeated the Tatars. Ivan the Great, however, inherited a state weakened by many years of oppressive rule. Russia had fallen far behind the rest of Europe when it came to advances in technology, scholarship, the arts, and social organization.

After Ivan the Great's rule, Russia descended once again into confusion and disorganization. For many years, the country suffered under poor government. The Poles and Swedes invaded but were eventually driven back by a national uprising. Finally, in 1613, Michael Romanov was crowned tsar, and although he wasn't a particularly strong leader, Russia stabilized. The Romanov lineage would remain the Russian royal family until their eventual overthrow in 1917.

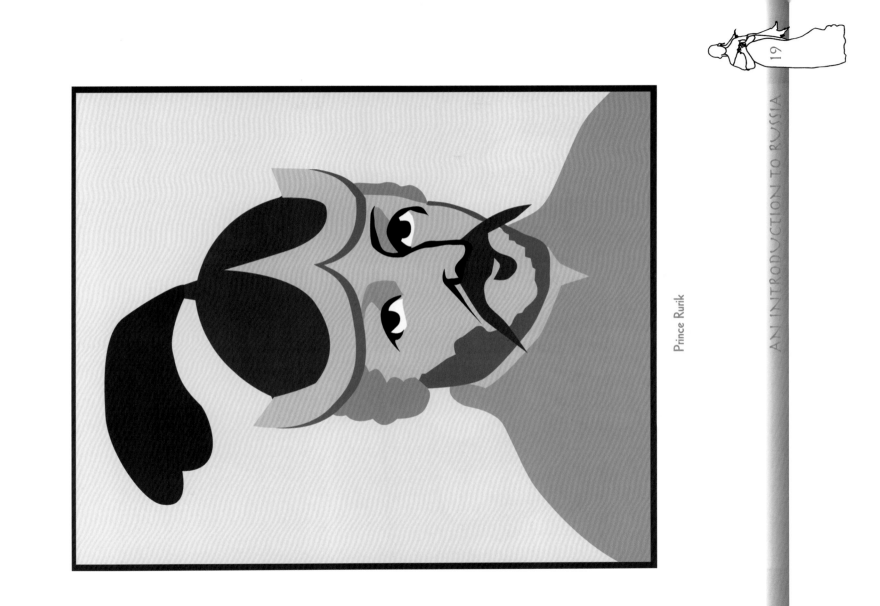

Prince Rurik

Peter the Great

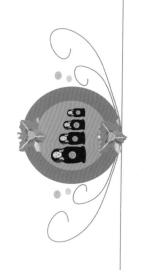

Ivan the Great was the first Russian ruler to call himself tsar, a term meant to indicate that the right to rule was divine, or given by the authority of God.

Under Michael Romanov and his successor, the borders of the Russian state expanded, driven largely by the fur trade. At this time, Russia's borders were marked by Poland in the west and the Ural Mountains in the east, but fur-bearing animals west of the Ural Mountains were disappearing. Hungry for more furs, Russians crossed into the Siberian forests east of the Ural Mountains. The tsars helped the traders by sending armies to conquer the people already living in the region. Russia's eastward expansion steamed ahead, reaching the Pacific Ocean in 1648. Subsequently, the border was extended southwards to China.

One of Russia's most important leaders was Peter the Great. He was the first monarch to institute modernizing policies by founding schools, libraries, and an academy of sciences. He also ordered the building of a new capital city, St. Petersburg, which became Russia's capital in 1712. The reign of Peter the Great was marked by war, a pattern followed by his successors, and borders shifted as land was won and lost.

Despite some gains in areas like education, the Russian government and aristocracy continued their oppression of the Russian people. Serfdom had been abolished in much of Europe, but it continued and grew harsher in Russia.

Only wealthy people had political influence, and anyone who disagreed with government policies or upset the ruling parties could be executed or banished to Siberia. The average Russian person had virtually no freedom in society and no voice in government. The social problems of having a large, oppressed group of people living in poverty plagued the state.

Though distrust of the government brewed at home, Russia continued its imperial expansion. In 1904, war broke out with the Japanese. A year later, Russia suffered a disastrous defeat, and discontent swirled among the population. A protest against the government's policies took place, and the situation turned disastrous when troops opened fire on the crowd, killing two hundred people and wounding hundreds more. The day came to be called "Bloody Sunday," and from that day forward, the Russian population marched steadily toward revolution.

The situation became even less stable during World War I, which spanned the years 1914 to 1918 and involved many countries. Russia aligned with France, Britain, Canada, the United States, and others in opposition to Germany.

By 1917, the government was no longer able to contain the discontent that resulted from the killing and starvation associated with war. The tsar was overthrown and a *liberal* provisional government assumed power. This government only lasted eight months before the Bolsheviks, a group of *communists* led by Vladimir Ilyich Ulyanov (later known as Lenin), seized power. It was the first Communist Revolution in the world. Under communism, everyone had to fulfill what was known as a "universal labor obligation." This meant you had to work for the state with no pay. In return, the state was supposed to give you food, housing, medical care, and education.

Russia negotiated an end to the war with Germany in 1918, relinquishing huge areas along its western border. Some territories, such as Ukraine, Belarus, and Georgia rejoined Russia and formed the Union of Soviet Socialist

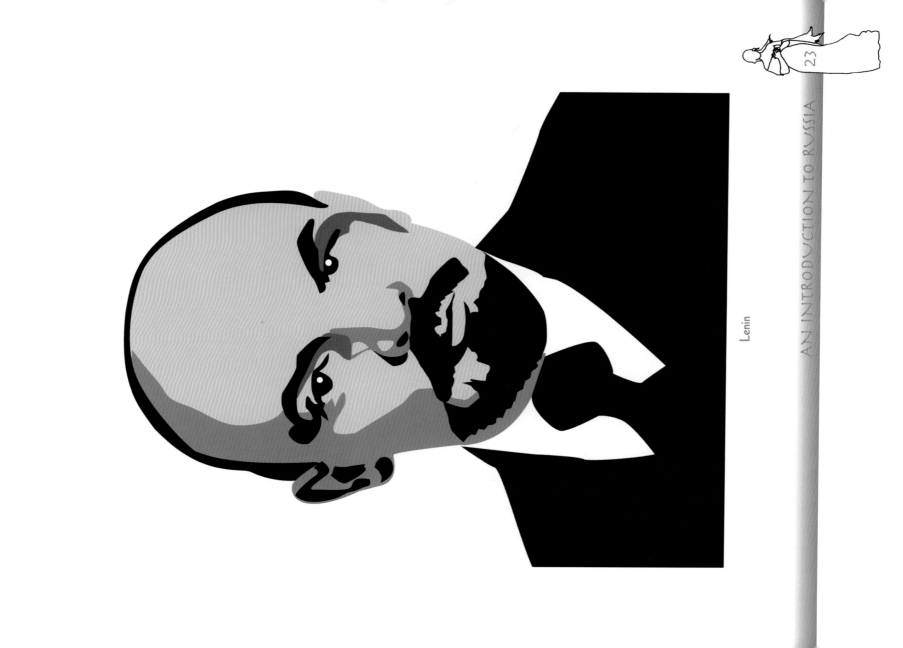

Lenin

Republics (USSR) in 1922. Lithuania, Estonia, Moldova, Poland, Czechoslovakia, Hungary, Romania, and Bulgaria would be seized by the Soviet Union after World War II.

After Lenin's death in 1924, a new age of terror began in the Soviet Union under the leadership of Joseph Stalin. One of Stalin's most devastating policies was collectivization. The state seized all farmland from private owners, then forced the people to farm the land collectively and turn all the produce over to the government. The government would then redistribute the food to citizens. People caught saving food for themselves or their family faced harsh punishment, even execution. Collectivization devastated the people of the Soviet Union, and six to ten million people starved to death in Ukraine in one year alone.

The rest of the world, however, would not know about the atrocities in the Soviet Union for many years. The government strictly regulated all information, and even many people within the Soviet Union did not know how bad the

During the First World War, the Russian economic situation was so bleak that the country could barely equip its soldiers. Between 1914 and 1915, half of the Russian reinforcements were sent to the front lines without even having rifles.

Joseph Stalin

Nikita Krushchev

situation was. As Winston Churchill remarked, "From Stettin in the Baltic to Trieste in the Adriatic an iron curtain has descended across the Continent." Behind this "iron curtain," Stalin killed those who opposed him and sent millions more to their deaths in a system of work camps called the *gulag*. By 1949, the Soviet Union had developed its own atomic bomb (the United States had developed one during World War II) and became deeply entrenched in a period of distrust and hostility with the West. This uncertain period was known as the Cold War. For decades, the United States and the Soviet Union faced each other, nuclear weapons armed and hands poised nervously over the controls.

After Stalin's death in 1953, Nikita Khrushchev became the new leader of the Soviet Union. Great oppression, especially of religious organizations, occurred during Khrushchev's leadership as well. But Khrushchev was not, in most ways, as brutal as Stalin, and conditions improved for much of the population. Khrushchev even attempted to bring more democracy to the Soviet Union, but his thinking wasn't in line with the rest of the Communist Party's, and he was eventually pushed out of his leadership role because of his efforts.

The nuclear arsenals of the Soviet Union and the United States continued to grow, but the Soviet Union was faltering under economic strains. In 1985, then leader of Russia, Secretary General Mikhail Gorbachev, instituted a policy of governmental reform called perestroika that included openness with the West called glasnost. Gorbachev was attempting to end the Cold War. The changes brought more democratic ideas to Russia, but made Gorbachev incredibly unpopular with his party.

In 1991, the Communist Party placed Gorbachev and his family under house arrest and staged a *coup*. In the West, people held their breath as they watched the dramatic events unfold in the news. In a scene that will be remembered around the world, future leader Boris Yeltsin climbed aboard one of the tanks, stood in full range of snipers, and called to the people of Russia to resist the coup, denounce the Communist system, and embrace democracy. Apparently moved by Yeltsin's words, some of the tanks turned around to protect the leader they had been ordered to overthrow, and the coup failed.

Upon his release, Gorbachev resigned and disbanded the Communist Party. On December 25, 1991, the Soviet Union dissolved, Eastern European countries like Ukraine and Belarus gained their independence, and Russia's borders receded to their present locations.

Today, Russia's capital is once again located in the city of Moscow. Russia now has a freely elected president and a young *capitalist system*. Much of Russia's economy is based on the extraction, processing, and export of raw materials like coal, oil, wood, and various metals. Crops like potatoes, sugar beets, sunflowers, grains, and vegetables are also important to the country.

The United Nations estimates the 2005 population of Russia to be approximately 141,553,000 people with the vast majority of the population living in urban areas. According to the UN's estimates, nearly 73 percent of Russia's people live in or around cities, and only 27 percent live in rural areas. During the Communist era, people could not own their own land; everything was owned by the government and then given to the people for their use. For this reason, most city dwellers today live in small apartments that were granted to their families during the communist era. Few people have land in the country or own individual houses.

The population of Russia is shrinking, with the average woman having only 1.14 children. Life expectancy in Russia is also quite low compared to other industrialized nations. The average life expectancy for women is 73 years, and the average life expectancy for men is only 61.2 years. Though now

Mikhail Gorbachev

Modern Russia still faces many challenges.

a democracy, Russia faces economic, social, and political challenges that at times seem insurmountable. Life in Russia continues to be extremely difficult for most people. Women make up a majority of the Russian population (more than 53 percent) and play an extremely important role in all aspects of life in the country today.

"SHE SITS BEHIND THREE-TIMES-NINE LOCKS; SHE SITS BEHIND THREE-TIMES-NINE KEYS; WHERE THE WIND NEVER BLEW, THE SUN NEVER SHONE, AND YOUNG HEROES NEVER SAW HER."
—AN ACCOUNT OF THE TEREM BY NATALIA PUSHKAREVA

2

WOMEN IN RUSSIA THROUGHOUT HISTORY

Throughout history, women's contributions to society have often been over-looked and underappreciated. Many people think that women have always been relegated to the home, forced to be subservient to men, and therefore haven't done much of consequence. This is completely untrue! Women's work, both in-side and outside of the home, has been extremely important to the development of societies and should not be dropped from the pages of history. In chapter 1, we reviewed some of the major events in Russia's development. Now we'll take a closer look at these time periods to discover how women participated in these events and what their lives were like.

Russian society has historically been patriarchal, meaning that men governed the society and family lines were traced through males. Russian households were made up of extended families. A typical household contained the eldest male, his wife, their sons, and their sons' wives and children. The eldest male was the official head, or patriarch, of the household. The eldest woman was also

Russian women have a long tradition of needlecraft.

an important authority figure. She oversaw the daily management of the household and had authority over the children and other relatives.

In early times in Eurasia, women's lives were defined by the activities of the home. Life was very different from today, and the daily maintenance of a household meant backbreaking work from pre-dawn until after dusk. Women ground flour, baked bread, fetched water (there was no such thing as going to the store for food or turning on a faucet for water), preserved and stored food, spun thread, made clothing, and labored in the fields. It took great expertise to make the beautiful linens that were common in Russia, and girls began learning this art at an early age. By the time a woman was ready to marry, she would already have learned the skills necessary to run a household.

Russian men were clearly the heads of their families, but the knowledge that came with overseeing the daily running of a household often made it necessary for women to handle the finances and budget. Women's expertise with budgets and financial management sometimes led husbands to entrust the family's wealth, and even important business dealings to their wives. These responsibilities were even more common among women of the upper classes who had greater access to education, property, and wealth.

In some ways, there was more equality and freedom in the early Russian state than in other parts of Europe. Members of the peasant classes had more freedom of movement. Serfdom had not yet seized the peasant population, and they could buy, sell, and inherit land. In Rus, although there was a grand prince to whom everyone paid tribute, local assemblies governed towns, and free men could call a meeting any time by ringing the town bell. The power of convening local meetings, however, did not extend to women. Nevertheless, there were laws that gave Russian women certain rights their European counterparts did not have. Most important among these was the right to own land.

Landowners in Rus had great influence in the government, and women who owned large amounts of land were also influential, sometimes to the point of achieving equality with men. In other parts of Europe at the time, women were barred from owning property, but in the Russian state, a woman entered into a marriage with a dowry, a portion of goods, property, or land.

Dowries were by no means unique to Russia, but what was unique was the fact that a woman's dowry did not become the property of her husband or in-laws. According to Russian historian Natalia Pushkareva, a Russian woman maintained control over her dowry after marriage and could buy, sell, or otherwise use her property without her husband's interference.

Another unique aspect of Russian property laws was that in the event of divorce or widowhood, the woman retained her land holdings. These laws were meant to protect women from poverty. If a woman's husband died or divorced

Not all women in pre-Russia worked specifically in the domestic sphere. In the second century C.E., the elite forces of the Sarmatian army contained both men and women. The Sarmatians were the dominant group living in the Black Sea region in this time period. This tells us that, at least in some areas of pre-Russia, women could occupy the same roles as men, even in the military.

her, she would still have a place to live and land to farm. Furthermore, upon being widowed, a woman could control her underage children's inheritance and make decisions on their behalf. In other patriarchal societies, these decision-making powers and the control of estates passed over the mother to an adult male relative.

Women, however, were still far from having complete freedom in Rus. A woman's ability to acquire wealth still depended upon marriage, for it was only in marriage that she would receive her dowry. If widowed, women could inherit additional land and property from their husbands, but daughters only inherited land from their fathers if there was no male heir. Sons inherited all the land and were expected to give their sisters an appropriate dowry when they married. It wasn't until the thirteenth century that laws were changed to give daughters equal inheritance rights. Furthermore, though some laws protected women's rights to property, a husband still had power over his wife's life. For example, a husband could state in his will whether or not his wife could remarry. Often a husband ordered his wife to enter a convent upon his death. If a husband made this command, a woman could do nothing to change her fate. The Orthodox Church, in fact, played a large role in maintaining women's secondary standing in Russian society.

According to Orthodox Christianity, a woman should be passive, humble, virtuous, and always submissive toward her husband. Religions play an important role in the development of societies and culture, and Orthodox beliefs became well-ingrained in Russia.

A woman can actually be given credit for the state's conversion to Orthodox Christianity. Perhaps the first Russian to convert to Christianity was Olga, the grandmother of Emperor Vladimir I. She had been converted in 957 B.C.E. in Constantinople, and is sometimes credited with her grandson's conversion from

The Orthodox Church has provided many Russian women with strength, even while it has helped to maintain women's secondary position in Russian culture.

the area's traditional *animist* religion, but the Emperor's conversion involved another important woman as well.

Curious about the world's religions, Vladimir sent a group of wise men to investigate different practices around the world. The delegation returned to Russia, most impressed with what they had seen in Greece, and gave a vivid description of Greek Orthodox Christianity. In 988 B.C.E., Vladimir set out for Greece, where he besieged the city of Kherson and sent a message to the Emperor of Constantinople, Basil, threatening to conquer another Greek city if he was not permitted to marry Basil's sister, Princess Anna. Basil replied that it was impossible for a Christian to marry a pagan; if Vladimir wanted to marry Anna, he would have to convert to Christianity and be baptized. Vladimir agreed.

At first Anna did not want to go, but she finally agreed after her brothers convinced her that in marrying Vladimir she would be bringing Christianity to Russia. In Vladimir's time, little religious tolerance existed in Russian society. People were expected to convert to their ruler's religion. As soon as Vladimir was baptized, he married Anna, and they returned to Kiev where the church was established as the official religion of the state.

Anna's role in Russia's conversion to Christianity may seem passive by today's standards, but in the male-dominated world of tenth-century Russia, women affected changes in ways that are different from today. Women's influence was still important; it just occurred in more indirect ways than it occurs in the twenty-first century. On occasion, however, some women rose up and had much more direct influence through leadership in government.

In Rus, marriages were an important part of politics. Russian princesses were well-educated, and those who married abroad often had more education than their new husbands and were at an advantage for gaining influence in foreign

governments. This situation benefited the Russian state. Many Russian princesses who married men from other countries used their influence with their husbands to further Russian interests.

From the eleventh to the fourteenth centuries, princesses in Rus often ruled alongside their husbands, playing important advisory and even decision-making

A Russian icon portraying the Christian concept of the Trinity.

roles. Several women rose up to lead on their own, often after their husband's death, but occasionally by actually overthrowing their husband's government.

One example of a woman leader in Russia is Anna Romanovna who led the principality of Galich after her husband's death. In the twelfth century, she formed strong international ties with Hungary, Lithuania, and Poland. She was forced to flee to Poland, however, when the *boyars* who opposed her seized power. But Anna would not easily be unseated. For nearly forty years, she planned and gained support for her return. Then, with the help of the Hungarian army, she re-seized her throne, arresting all those who had opposed her. She ruled until 1214 when she passed the thrown on to her son.

Like Anna, most Russian and European women had to take a backdoor to leadership through a male. Women were not raised to be heirs and leaders the way men were. Only through marriage, motherhood, and other family ties to men did women find their way to leadership in Russia, and most women who ascended to the throne did so in the name of their underage sons. This did not, however, prevent them from being important and influential leaders.

Not all women who rose to power in the state of Rus, however, met success or happy endings. Leadership in the Russian state was highly coveted and highly contested. Conspiracies were common, and leaders were frequently overthrown. Female leaders faced even more problems. Most people disapproved of female leadership, and supporters could not be trusted to remain loyal. Women leaders were frequently overthrown and banished to convents, where they were forced to take vows as nuns. A number of strong women who resisted designs on their leadership were poisoned.

Beginning with the invasion of the Tatar army in the thirteenth century, women's position in Russia steadily declined. Under Mongol rule, all of Russia became less politically active. Russia's main focus at this time was paying trib-

A modern Russian wedding.

ute to their Mongol overlords, and contact with the rest of Europe was cut off. The politically advantageous marriages Russian women had once enjoyed abroad came to a halt, and thus women were stripped of their main avenue to power.

Under Tatar rule, most women of the privileged classes began to devote themselves completely to household and family matters. Some women, however, refused to be intimidated by the Tatar leadership. Princess Ksenia of Iaroslavl and her daughter Maria are examples. In 1288, while Maria's husband, Prince Fedor Rostislavich, was away seeking permission from the Khan to rule his principality and was being wooed by the Khan's daughter, Ksenia and Maria staged a revolt. They placed Fedor's underage son Mikhail on the thrown and then ruled in his name.

Fedor, outraged, married the Khan's daughter, and the Khan demanded that Ksenia and Maria relinquish the thrown. Neither woman, however, would bow to the Khan's demands or threats. As rulers, they had strong support from the local population, and they maintained their power. Eventually, however, after Ksenia, Maria, and Mikhail had all died, Fedor returned to Iaroslavl and re-claimed his thrown.

One might expect that women's situation in Russia improved after the end of Tatar rule, but in fact the opposite happened. In the sixteenth and seventeenth centuries, women of the upper classes quickly lost influence as a new practice was introduced: secluding women in the terem, or the women's quarters of the house. In the terem, women could be literally kept behind lock and key. Even secluded women who were not literally locked up were still not permitted to go out in public, and all of their visitors were screened for appropriateness.

The stated purpose for secluding women was for protection. Apparently by being locked away, women would be safe from invaders or people who wished

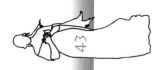

to insult their honor. The terem, however, also served other purposes that were useful to the government and church. It prevented wives from having affairs or engaging in political conspiracies; it assured that daughters would remain virgins until marriage; and it isolated women from the affairs of state, making it more difficult for them to attain positions of leadership.

Seclusion in the terem, however, only affected women of the upper classes, for only wealthy people could afford to lock half the people capable of doing work behind impenetrable walls. In fact, some of the most notable women of the time period came from the peasant classes. One such woman was Alena Arzamasskaia.

Pushkareva tells Alena's story in *Women in Russian History*. In the 1660s and '70s, many peasant revolts took place in Russia. Alena, a peasant woman who had fled her life as a nun, led one of these rebellions. Posing as a man, she collected a small regiment. But as Alena's reputation grew, so too did her army, swelling to six thousand strong. They conquered the city of Temnikov. Alena had proved herself a good leader and established her rule over the city.

In just a few months, however, the tsar's army bore down on Temnikov. Alena's forces fought but were overcome, and Alena was captured. Under torture, she refused to give the identities of other rebel leaders. For her impunity, defection from the convent, leadership of the revolt, and impersonation of a man (considered by many to be the worst of her crimes), she was sentenced to death by burning at the stake.

In the seventeenth century, the practice of seclusion in the terem began to fade, and women trickled back into political life. In the late eighteenth century, Catherine the Great took the throne. Catherine was an extremely active politician, and had engaged in a conspiracy, lured the military to her side, and then seized power while her husband was traveling abroad. There was strong support for Catherine's new government, and she ruled from 1762 to 1796.

A modern Russian woman earns her living as a street sweeper.

Modern-day Russians crowd Moscow's busy Arbat Street.

Many historical accounts of Catherine's leadership focus only on her numerous relationships with men, and completely ignore the fact that Catherine was a great modernizer and reformer. She introduced many of the ideas of the European *Enlightenment*. She spoke fluent French and made it the language of the court. She used skillful military planning and diplomacy to regain most of the territories that Peter the Great lost, and under her leadership, Russia became one of the Great Powers of Europe.

Catherine's powerful rule, however, did not always have positive effects. After the French Revolution, she clamped down on the press in Russia and ordered *francophones* to be placed under surveillance. Furthermore, after a failed serf rebellion, Catherine introduced the practice of exiling political opponents to Siberia. This practice continued well into the twentieth century under Communist Party rule.

"[Alena] did not express any fear, or even make a sound, when she was entirely enveloped in flames."

—spoken by an eyewitness to Alena's execution and quoted in Pushkareva's **Women in Russian History**

Under the Communists, drastic societal reforms took place almost immediately. Communism had various, sometimes conflicting, effects on women's lives. On the one hand, educational and career opportunities were opened up to women. Women began to work outside of the home in greater numbers and in different types of jobs. They were given the right to vote. The state provided some basic day-care services, free abortions, and guarantees for child support from husbands in the event that a couple divorced. When Josef Stalin came to power, he instituted a policy of forced *industrialization* and *modernization*. Millions of people were needed to work in the new factories and mines of Russia. As a result, more opportunities opened up as the state built new factories and mines. Education became free for those who earned entrance into the state-controlled universities. In the 1930s, some women were even given a stipend to finish high school or go to a university.

But the Communist era did not bring about full equality for women. The opportunities that developed for women were often different from the opportunities that developed for men. Furthermore, these so-called opportunities occurred alongside universal labor obligations. State policy also ensured that women held lower paying positions. While many women became doctors and engineers, professions traditionally held by men, most managerial positions were retained by men. Furthermore, services designed to ease the domestic burden of working women, like day-care, were scarce, and women struggled to balance their work inside and outside the home.

Women's work outside the home increased, but their roles in the home did not diminish. They were expected to continue fulfilling the traditional household responsibilities of wives and mothers. The domestic sphere was still regarded as a female sphere. Stalin's policies made women's responsibilities even harder to fulfill. With the collectivized farms, women could do little to keep

Catherine the Great

their families from starving. To make matters worse, most of the people Stalin had exiled or killed were men. Many of these men left families behind, and women were left as the sole supporters for these families, both financially and emotionally.

When the Second World War broke out in 1939, many women served in the Russian army as doctors, nurses, pilots, and snipers. They also formed the majority of factory workers. By 1946, after the war had ended, Stalin's violent policies coupled with the casualties of war had produced a population imbalance. There were over 25 million more women than men.

A modern statue in Moscow recognizes women's role in the Russian economy.

During the Cold War, the government constantly prepared the Russian people for war with the Western countries in Europe and North America. During this period, women continued to work in jobs like engineering and physics, jobs that required high levels of education. However, they also continued to live in a patriarchal society that viewed women as best behaved when submissive and showing deference to men.

"THE BIRD THAT WOULD SOAR ABOVE THE LEVEL PLAIN OF TRA-DITION AND PREJUDICE MUST HAVE STRONG WINGS."
—KATE CHOPIN

WOMEN IN RUSSIA TODAY

3

In Russian society today, echoes of the past are everywhere and often collide with present conditions, values, and beliefs. Women in Russia are a diverse group, and it would be misleading to say that their experiences are all the same. It is safe to say, however, that women in Russia today are experiencing a mix of losses and gains.

Today, women make up a majority of the Russian workforce, something they have done since Stalin's devastating era. Since the collapse of Communism in 1991, rapid changes have occurred in Russia. In some ways, these changes are positive, and women are experiencing the effects of more freedom. Many now work in prestigious positions as economists, interpreters, intelligence officers, business owners, doctors, lawyers, policewomen, and university professors. Today, young people in Russia have more opportunities than the older generation had when they were growing up.

Women are important to the new economy not only as workers but also as consumers. A capitalist economy depends largely upon the demand for and the sale of goods and services. There are now more consumer goods available to Russians. Women are often the ones who are responsible for making the decisions about buying the goods needed for their household. However, the Russian people's ability to support a capitalist, consumer-based economy is undermined by a lack of wealth and job security.

Despite the fact that some women have made great strides in the workforce, they still struggle with wage inequality. On average, women earn one-third less than men for the same work. In fact, there is a *correlation* between the movement toward higher salaries in a given position and a decline in the number of women employed in that field. This problem plagues women into their futures, as lower salaries also mean women get less of a pension when they retire.

Commuters crowd one of Moscow's subway stops.

Even very well-educated women often find that they can only get hired for low-skill, low-paying work, a phenomenon known as underemployment. In fact, most department heads in research institutes, government agencies, and corporations are men. Though numerous women are professionally employed, few women can attain promotion to managerial positions. This problem is not unique to Russia. It happens in numerous countries all over the world and is often referred to as the "glass ceiling," meaning that women can see how to advance in their employment, have fulfilled all the requirements for that advancement, are capable of holding the job, yet find an invisible barrier separating them from the men at the top.

Even women who are underemployed in Russia, however, often consider themselves lucky, for many other women have lost their jobs completely. With the collapse of the Communist system came the collapse of the state-regulated economy. Throughout the Communist era, the Soviet government spent huge amounts of money and resources creating and maintaining jobs. When the system, no longer able to sustain the costs of artificially created jobs, finally fell, many people were laid off.

Women are the first to get laid off in Russia. Though making up the majority of the workforce, women also account for about two-thirds of Russia's unemployed. In Russian society, men are usually considered the main providers for a family, and married women are therefore laid off before men. In Russia, staff cuts are clearly made on the basis of gender, not merit.

Some women have taken the problem of being underemployed or unemployed and turned it around by becoming independent *entrepreneurs*. Women now comprise 70 percent of all merchants in the outdoor markets. Many of these women are highly educated. Some have degrees in physics and chemical engineering. Others were university professors. These women are selling goods because they lost their jobs or were being paid such ridiculously small salaries that they could not afford to keep their previous employment and decided to strike out on their own.

Newly independent female entrepreneurs face additional challenges in a society so dominated by men. Often banks refuse to give loans to women. In response, women's business groups have formed and help each other to secure credit. The support network of these groups also helps women make the connections needed for success in capitalism. This has helped reduce the effects of male entrepreneurs who are hesitant to do business with women. It also gives emotional support to help women overcome problems of low self-confidence.

An example of one of these business groups is the Russian Women's Microfinance Network (RWMN). Chaired by businesswoman Diana Medman, the Microfinance Network, with the help of Women's World Bank, has been assisting women in business since 1998. Groups like RWMN can be seen as part of a growing women's movement in Russia.

Building a women's movement in Russia has proven to be a challenge. During communism, people could not freely associate in groups. The soviet government was extremely paranoid, and any non-government or non-Communist organization was suspected of anti-state activities. People accused of plotting against the state could be exiled to the gulag, imprisoned in a work camp, or executed with little or no evidence. The Soviet population was closely monitored by the government, and only state-approved or state-sponsored organizations were allowed to meet.

Since the fall of Communism, great strides have been made as free speech and freedom of association have taken hold. Today, there are over fifty groups devoted to women's issues. Nevertheless, challenges still exist. There are numerous echoes from Soviet times in current Russian society, and the country still faces threats to democracy. There are also reactions from patriarchal structures within society. Yet as collaboration between groups increases their influence, the effects on Russian politics and policy-making becomes more pronounced.

These Russian women earn their living selling fruit to passersby.

A Russian woman looks for opportunities posted on a Moscow kiosk.

During the Communist era, an organization of secret policy, called the KGB, were in charge of investigating and crushing any attempts at "counterrevolution." The KGB had secret agents in every level of society, watching for anti-government activities. The KGB had great power, and "convinced" people to support the government by threatening their jobs and families, evicting them from their homes, subjecting people to torture, and sending people to the gulag.

Many of the women's groups are non-governmental organizations (NGOs) that offer educational, career, and social services. These organizations give women a support network, helping them deal with some of the emotional and financial challenges that have come with life in the new Russia. Like RWMN, some of these organizations help women start their own businesses, while others support women in the arts. Some groups council women on how to get further in their careers, while others provide crisis services for problems like drug abuse, alcoholism, and domestic violence. Some of the organizations are part of huge, international women's groups, while others are small and operate only in their local community. No matter what their form, many of these organizations are fulfilling a valuable function by filling a void left by a cash-strapped government as it cuts social services and other financial resources that had previously benefited women and families.

Russian women come together to help each other.

Even though numerous women's organizations operate in Russia, it would be inaccurate to say that Russia is currently undergoing a feminist movement like the one experienced in the United States in the late 1960s and early '70s. In fact, many Russian women do not even desire such a movement and wish to retain control of their traditional roles as wives and mothers. This does not, however, mean that women generally prefer to remain subordinate to men and have fewer opportunities than their male counterparts.

Despite a decade of trying to foster a change in attitudes, traditional *stereotypes* prevail. The *Christian Science Monitor* reports a survey in which Russian men and women were asked to name what they regarded as a woman's role. Those that responded stated predominantly traditional views. Forty-eight percent of all respondents cited "mother" as a woman's role. The next most commonly cited role was "businesswoman," at 18 percent, but following close behind was "wife," with 17 percent. A full 11 percent of respondents said a woman's role was as "housekeeper." "Politician," on the other hand, the embodiment of political empowerment, was cited by a mere 1 percent of respondents. While it is encouraging that the second largest response was for businesswoman, an example of an economically empowered individual, it lags far behind that of the traditional role of woman as mother and is nearly tied with wife. The almost nonexistent response for politician closely reflects the realities of Russian society.

Literacy rates are an important indicator of a population's education level. According to United Nations statistics, Russia has extremely high literacy rates. In fact, its literacy rates are some of the highest in the world. Girls and boys in Russia have equal access to education, yet the UN's statistics show a slight disparity in literacy, with 100 percent for boys but only 97 percent for girls. Nevertheless, this is a dramatic improvement from before the Communist era, when over 85 percent of women could not read or write. The reason for the gap between female and male literacy rates is probably accounted for by the number of older women who were denied education as youths in the earlier era.

In some ways, schooling in Russia today resembles the education system before the collapse of the Soviet Union. Attendance at school is mandatory for the first eight years. After this, there is an option to study for a further two. Upon graduating at age seventeen, a student can apply to a university. Many of the best universities are in the western part of the country in St. Petersburg and Moscow. More girls than boys choose to graduate. As a result, it is not common for women to be better educated than men.

The types of subjects taught in Russian schools has changed somewhat. For example, during Communist times, children were taught military training in preparation for a possible attack from the United States, the Cold War enemy. Schoolchildren, including girls, were taught how to take apart and clean a gun, as well as how to throw a grenade! (Of course, the "grenade" was usually a potato.) Today, this course is not part of a child's education. The sciences, math, Russian, and English were also taught before the end of Communism, and today these are the dominant subjects.

Girls and boys often have different experiences growing up in Russia. One woman who grew up in the ship-building center of Vladivostok explained what it is like to be a girl in Russia. "Growing up in Russia, there is a lot more pressure," she said. "You are supposed to be a model child. There is a lot of pressure to be a perfect child. With the girls it was more so. With the boys it was often said that they did not know any better, but if you were a girl, it was always pointed out that you were a girl and that more was expected of you. People would say, 'You should know better, you are a girl.'"

Despite sometimes being treated differently, girls growing up in Russia today generally feel that they have as many opportunities as boys have. Russian

A bustling indoor market where Russians can purchase fresh produce.

Visitors to Lenin's tomb in Moscow's Red Square.

people have long understood that the key to advancement in society and a better life is education. Equal education for girls and boys is one area in which Russia has made great strides, and access to a good education is what gives many people hope for the future.

However, the country's economic troubles have even affected the education system. Russia's universities, once sources of so much pride for the Russian people, have suffered under extreme budget cuts and lost faculty. Some universities' facilities have greatly declined. For these reasons, the few families who can afford to do so often send their children to study abroad.

"AT WORK, YOU THINK OF THE
CHILDREN YOU'VE LEFT AT HOME.
AT HOME, YOU THINK OF THE WORK
YOU'VE LEFT UNFINISHED. SUCH A
STRUGGLE IS UNLEASHED WITHIN
YOURSELF, YOUR HEART IS RENT."
—GOLDA MEIR (1898–1978), RUSSIAN-
BORN ISRAELI PRIME MINISTER

4

WOMEN AND THE FAMILY

Numerous challenges face Russian families today. Most of these challenges arise from complications associated with poor economic conditions. Throughout the world, it is a sad truth that in times of economic hardship, it is often women and children who suffer the most. Women, as the main caretakers of households, children, the sick, and the elderly often have less freedom of movement than men. They cannot simply pick up and move to a place where there is more work, and they have greater constraints on their time. Even when a woman can find enough time for duties both within and outside of the home, her quality of life decreases. Nevertheless, economic conditions usually leave women with no choice about working outside of the home. The situation can be worse for single women, of which there are many in Russia, who must be the sole support for their families. Furthermore, the difficulty in balancing working life with home life is only one of the challenges facing Russian families.

Today, forty million Russians live in poverty. This is slightly less than one in three people. To make matters worse, Russia has a housing crisis. Most people

A Russian woman sits with her baby in a St. Petersburg park.

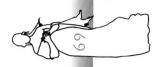

still live in large housing blocks left over from the Soviet era. These are massive apartment buildings, and each individual unit is often too small for the needs of a given family. The shortage in the supply of housing means that many Russians live in an extended family situation, with a couple of generations living together under one roof. Couples who have children will live with one of the grandparents in an undersized apartment.

This cramped living situation can be difficult for everyone involved. Most apartments only have one or two small bedrooms. With three generations under one roof, there usually aren't enough bedrooms for all, and the family sofa often serves in Russian households as a grandparent's or child's bed. Furthermore, in the Soviet era, many apartments didn't even have their own bathrooms or kitchens. Instead, one bathroom and one kitchen were shared by a number of apartments. Today, fewer people suffer with these problems, but some still live with such sharing arrangements.

Cramped as it may be, however, most families find it absolutely necessary to live in multigenerational households. Not only would it be impossible to afford anything else, but with both parents working to make ends meet, and with few options for affordable day-care, a grandparent in the home fills the needed role of child-care provider.

The economic strain of the shift to a market economy has resulted in another change in family structure. Families in Russia have recently been shrinking in size. Russian women on average now have only 1.14 children. Such a low birthrate has caused a problem in Russia: more people die each year than there are babies being born. Russia's population is therefore shrinking. In fact, although today there are 141 million Russians, by 2010, the United Nations estimates that the population of Russia will fall to 137 million.

A falling population is a symptom of a number of problems and social challenges that Russian women face. The obvious one is that Russian families are less able to afford to have children. Another reason for a low birthrate, however, is that Russia faces tremendous environmental degradation. Pollution levels are high in the land, water, and air, and this pollution has resulted in health problems like increased birth defects and higher infant mortality rates. Environmental problems can also lead to increased infertility in both men and women. Declining availability of healthcare has made these problems even worse. Increased disease, malnutrition, tobacco use, and alcohol consumption have also affected the number of healthy births.

Safe and effective birth control is also a problem for many Russian women. Low birth rates in most countries are usually indicative of women being highly educated about birth control and having adequate access to safe forms of contraception. In contemporary Russia, however, women do not have as much education about contraception and they have less access to birth control. Even women who are educated about safe contraception methods may not be able to afford them. In Russia, abortion often serves as a main form of birth control.

Abortions can pose serious health risks to women. If performed in the right medical facilities, abortions are generally safe, but healthcare in Russia has declined, and these services are not always available. Furthermore, infections after

For every ten live births in Russia, there are thirteen abortions. This is the second highest rate of abortion in the world after Romania.

Russian children sledding with their parents.

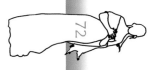

Some Russian women find hope for their problems in their faith. Here they have tied their prayer requests to a tree.

an abortion can cause long-term health risks and complications. The more abortions a woman has, the more risks there can be.

Today, there is a greater effort to make contraception available to women. This is also important because of the high HIV infection rates now being seen in Russia. HIV is the virus that causes AIDS and is a sexually transmitted disease. Using condoms during sex not only prevents pregnancy; it also prevents the spread of HIV.

In addition to the other difficulties facing families, domestic violence now affects more women in Russia than ever before. There are about 650,000 reported incidents of crimes against women each year in Russia. Part of the problem is deeply ingrained in the social fabric. Some men and women believe domestic abuse is a normal behavior. Recently, attempts have been made to change attitudes. Women's groups have an uphill battle, however, since educating men that abusive behavior is wrong is difficult in a society in which one old saying goes, "If he beats you, it means he loves you." Attempts to educate women have met with more success, and despite shortages in services like shelters for battered women, some advances have been made in providing other services, like crisis phone lines.

The problem of domestic violence is made worse by high unemployment and high levels of drug and alcohol abuse. Many unemployed people feel great frustration with their lives. Sometimes people, especially when using drugs or alcohol, take this frustration out on their spouses and children in the form of violence.

Most of the problems we have discussed are either directly or indirectly linked to the problems of poverty and a weak economy. Many people think that wealth will solve all of their problems. However, it may surprise you to learn that while poverty creates numerous difficulties for women in Russia, new wealth is causing some problems of its own.

A young Russian woman often faces many restrictions.

Wealthy Russians, the so-called New Russians, are a relatively recent phenomenon. People can choose to display (or not display) their wealth in many ways. Some people like fancy clothes, other people drive expensive cars. Some people collect rare art, and other people build huge houses. Some wealthy men in Russia have decided that a good way to show their wealth and status is to have a stay-at-home wife.

This belief provides disturbing echoes to the terem of the past, in which it was a status-symbol to keep the female family members locked away from public view—except these contemporary Russian women are not being protected from invaders or dishonor. They are being discouraged from working and are denied the independence that the market changes have made possible for Russian women. However, the idea of having a dependent wife who does not work to show your wealth and status is not at all unique to Russia or New Russians. It happens all over the world.

In some Russian families, both rich and poor, even women's role as consumers is curtailed as they are placed on an allowance, their household expenditures strictly budgeted. Women's groups in Russia have cited this as a distinct form of spousal abuse. It is not physical, but it is still *disempowering* and deeply threatens women's independence in these families.

"THE MORE PEOPLE WANT TO BE
FAITHFUL TO GOD, THE STRONGER
OUR COUNTRY WILL BE AND THE
LONGER IT WILL SURVIVE."
—KSENIYA, MOTHER SUPERIOR OF A
RUSSIAN ORTHODOX CONVENT

5

RELIGION'S ROLE IN THE LIVES OF RUSSIAN WOMEN

During the Soviet era, there was no such thing as religious freedom in Russia. Although in early times the Russian Orthodox Church was the official religion of the state and played an important role in government, during the communist era, the state was officially *atheistic*. Lenin proclaimed, "Every religious idea, every idea of a God, even flirting with the idea of a God is unspeakable vileness of the most dangerous kind." A huge effort was made to extinguish religion from the Soviet masses.

Today, many people in Russia are atheists. Growing up during the Communist era, they were rarely introduced to religion (except to have the idea denounced), and Communism took religion's place for many people. Communism was their faith and the Soviet Union was their church.

Today, however, there are still many others who retained their religious beliefs throughout Communist rule, even when doing so was dangerous to their safety or life. Some churches are experiencing a type of *renaissance* as the old practices are revived. In addition, church's religious ranks are swelling as more and more people look for meaning, hope, and a place of solace in the midst of their difficult and tumultuous lives. It is largely due to women that many religious communities and beliefs survived to be rediscovered today.

Today, the vast majority of religious Russians belong to the Russian Orthodox Church. The Russian Orthodox community suffered greatly under Soviet rule. During Stalin's reign, nearly all the country's churches, over 50,000 of them, were closed. Many were converted into factories or other uses for the state. Thousands of priest, bishops, nuns, and other faithful were sent to the gulag, and every monastery in the country (there had been more than one thousand) was emptied and closed.

To stay alive, the church pledged its support to the Soviet government and was able to continue some activities. The Soviet government, however, then had complete control over the church. They decided who was and was not able to become a priest and infiltrated the clergy with KGB spies. Some people, feeling betrayed by the Church's agreement with the state, broke away and formed their own underground church called the Church of the Catacombs. They worshiped secretly and attempted to keep the old beliefs alive.

The Soviet state's oppression of religious people continued until its fall in the 1990s. Religious leaders and freedom fighters were imprisoned, exiled, executed, and "treated" in psychiatric hospitals for their religious "sickness." Through this whole difficult era, Sunday schools and other forms of religious teaching were banned.

Journalist William Millinship explains in his book *Front Line: Women of the New Russia*, that one of the main reasons for the Church's survival was the staunch belief and determination of its women. Throughout history and in all parts of the world, women have played an important role in cultural transmission, or the passing on of beliefs, values, family history, and cultural practices from one generation to the next. In the Soviet situation, it was often grandmothers who stayed with the children while mothers worked. While young people were banned from attending church services, these elderly women could

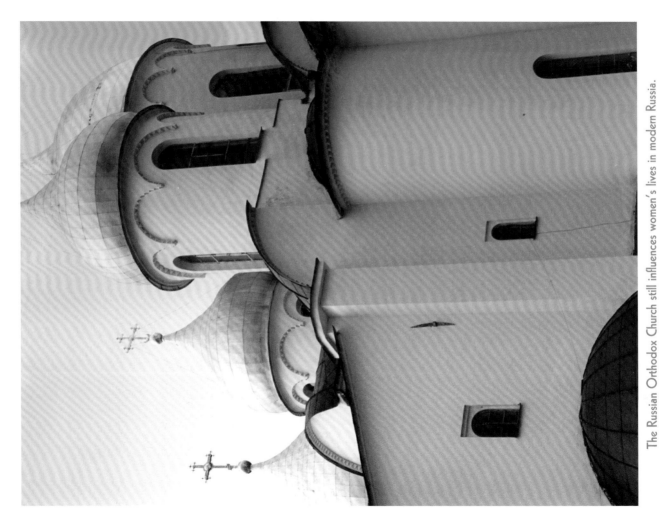

The Russian Orthodox Church still influences women's lives in modern Russia.

not be kept away and even crossed police lines to attend church. These grandmothers secretly passed religious teachings on to many of the country's youth.

The Russian Orthodox Church promotes a traditional role for women. According to its beliefs, women should be obedient wives and nurturing mothers. Women should retain their virginity until marriage and should be otherwise *pious* and virtuous. An example of a custom that Russian Orthodox women follow to demonstrate their feminine humility before God is the wearing of a head covering in church.

In 1 Corinthians 11:8–9 it states, "Indeed, man was not made from woman, but woman from man. Neither was man created for the sake of woman, but woman for the sake of man." Certainly not all Russian Orthodox women today would agree with this biblical teaching (taken out of context from the rest of the Bible's more positive teachings about women), but the Russian Orthodox Church continues to take this religious edict very literally. In fact, since its adoption in the ninth century, the Orthodox Church has played a key role in establishing and maintaining women's secondary status in Russian society. This is not to say that all, or even most, of Russian women disagree with the role the church promotes. In fact, many women as well as men, feel that the teachings of the Orthodox Church are quite correct in these matters.

✷ ✷ ✷

Today, Islam is the second most popular religion in Russia. Islam is a religion based on the teachings of the Prophet Muhammad who lived in the seventh century. People who practice Islam are called Muslims. They believe in one God whose name is Allah. Their holy scriptures are the Qur'an (also spelled Koran), but portions of the Judeo-Christian Bible are also important to Islamic tradition. The Islamic religion also promotes a traditional role for women and tends to be very strict about women's behavior and appearance.

Beginning with the tsars, the Muslim people of Russia were driven from their land and even faced *genocide*. Their oppression continues today. Many

Some Russian women demonstrate their devotion to the church with intricate handiwork like that displayed here.

A Christmas tree outside a church proclaims the religious freedom of twenty-first-century Russia.

Islamic people in Russia live in the region of Chechnya. Today, Chechnya is the focus of a very serious political and religious conflict. Chechnya declared but was not granted independence in the fall of the Soviet Union. A Chechen rebel army took up arms against Russia. Chechens have now endured a brutal occupation by Russian forces for more than ten years. The Russian soldiers have performed horrific human-rights abuses against the Chechen people, and thousands have died.

The conflict in Chechnya has had an alarming affect on some of the region's Muslim women. A now infamous group known as the Black Widows has risen. The Black Widows have been responsible for numerous suicide bombings in Moscow. In Chechnya and other contested areas, suicide bombings have become a common form of warfare for Islamic people. Before the emergence of the Black Widows, however, Islamic fighters and suicide bombers were almost always men. There are currently two theories about the unprecedented emergence of women as suicide bombers.

As more and more of their fathers, sons, husbands, and brothers have been killed by Russian soldiers, the women of Chechnya have become enraged. Some say that the Black Widows are women seeking revenge for the deaths of their husbands. According to another now popular theory, however, the Black Widows are not acting of their own volition, but are actually being used by terrorist groups. Some claim that the women are being forced into their deadly service as payment for family debts or to restore lost family honor.

At one time, Russia had the largest Jewish population in the world. However, Jewish people were not permitted to participate equally in Russian society. They were segregated in an area known as the Pale and were greatly persecuted. Later they were massacred in pogroms, organized campaigns carried out against the Jewish people. By the mid-twentieth century, millions of Russian Jews had been killed and many others had fled.

In the present day, Russian people are less frightened to claim their Jewish heritage. Nevertheless, few Jewish people in Russia actually practice their religion. This is because all of their religious activities had been banned, and many people never learned the religious practices of their heritage.

However, as with the Russian Orthodox religion, there are those who continued to secretly pass their faith on to their children. As one Russian woman remarked when discussing the religious rebirth that occurred in Russia after the fall of communism, "The more people I met, the more I realized how diverse it is. I met Jewish people I did not know were Jewish in Russia and now that they have emigrated to the States, they've told me about all the traditions they kept and holidays they always celebrated [throughout Communist rule]."

There are many different forms of Judaism, and they are not all the same, but in general Judaism tends to promote a great deal of equality between the sexes. In fact, it was a Russian-born Jewish woman, Golda Meir, who became the third female prime minister in the world. Golda Meir served as Prime Minister of Israel from 1969 to 1974 after occupying many other important government positions.

Although Russian Orthodox Christians, Muslims, and Jews are some of the largest religious groups in Russia today, other religions also exist. There are relatively small populations of Buddhists and Roman Catholics. Missionaries from various religions around the world have also become common. Mormon missionaries are especially numerous. Many people continue to feel perfectly happy without religious beliefs or affiliations, but for others, this new period has provided opportunities for finding hope, faith, and peace. Nevertheless, as the Black Widows show us with alarming clarity, religious conflicts have not ended in Russia, and unless the Russian government can find peaceful solutions, these conflicts will endure long into the future.

"EVERY WOMAN DREAMS
OF HER OWN POLITICAL CAREER
AND HER OWN PLACE IN LIFE."
—RAISA GORBACHEVA

OUTSTANDING RUSSIAN WOMEN

6

RAISA GORBACHEVA

For most of her adult life, Raisa Gorbacheva was loved abroad and despised at home. Born in Rubtsovsk, Siberia, in 1932, Raisa's young life, like that of many Russians, was marked by poverty and upheaval. Her grandfather had been arrested and then executed in the gulag. Her mother had very little education, only learning to read once she was an adult, and her father worked on the railway, which meant the family had to move often and sometimes live in carriages beside the railway tracks.

The struggles of her youth, however, would not stifle this young intellectual's abilities. From an early age, Raisa was clearly gifted with scholarly abilities. In her final year of high school, she achieved the highest marks possible in every single one of her subjects and thus won entrance to Moscow University, where she studied philosophy. At Moscow University, Raisa met her future husband, Mikhail Gorbachev, and they married two years later.

Early in their marriage, Raisa and Mikhail had their only child, Iriana. Raisa continued to study, eventually earning the Russian equivalent of a Ph.D., and

Another Russian leader, Alexandra Kollontai, was a major figure in her country's Socialist movement.

taught philosophy at the university level. When her husband became the leader of the Communist Party, Raisa and her family moved back to Moscow, where Raisa's political life grew dramatically.

Raisa Gorbacheva accompanied her husband on his first international travels as the Russian head of state, and her appearance on the world stage caused media sensations. She was clearly something the Western media had never seen before—a Russian woman who was smart, outspoken, stylish, and not afraid to be in the public eye. While the West fell in love with this "modern" woman, many in Russia scorned Raisa, focusing particularly on the fact that she wore designer clothing, something that did not in any way endear her to Russia's struggling masses.

The greatest source of Russia's bitterness toward their "First Lady," however, was Raisa's refusal to stay in the shadows. Unheard of among Kremlin wives, she attended press conferences, spoke openly on government matters, accompanied her husband on state visits, and was Mr. Gorbachev's closest advisor. In press conferences, her husband could even occasionally be seen consulting Raisa before commenting on an issue or answering a question, behavior that shocked and outraged many in the Russian public who felt a woman should never emerge from men's shadows. Gorbachev even stated openly in an American interview that he discussed everything with his wife, implying that he even discussed state matters with her. The statement was so shocking and unacceptable to the Soviet government that it was censored in the Soviet broadcast of the interview.

Though much attention was paid to Raisa Gorbacheva's clothes and style, her role in Russian government and world relations was much more important. Mikhail Gorbachev is credited with making the fall of the Soviet Union and warmer relations with the West possible, but Raisa Gorbacheva is often credited with giving the Soviet Union and leadership a "human face."

Sophia Kovalevskaya was a prominent Russian mathematician.

The Gorbachevs' lives were difficult after the fall of the Soviet Union. Though respected abroad, they were often treated as *pariahs* at home. Nevertheless, Raisa continued to work for charitable and humanitarian causes. In 1999, however, she was diagnosed with leukemia. Russia's view of Raisa took a dramatic shift. Suddenly, she was seen in a sympathetic light, as a modern woman who dared to show a new face on the world stage, as a woman who was able to balance political aspirations and familial love, and as a woman who helped to bring hope of a better future to Russia. Raisa, however, was never able to see if she could have a positive, lasting relationship with her fellow Russians. Her illness quickly grew worse, and on September 20, 1999, she died at the age of 67.

For years, Gorbachev's political adversaries encouraged rumors that Raisa squandered money on Parisian clothing (her clothing was actually made in Moscow). Raisa was often used as a symbol and **scapegoat** for the Soviet Union's economic problems. She was portrayed as reveling in a lavish (and state-funded) lifestyle, but in retrospect it seems that these charges were greatly inflated.

Raisa Gorbacheva's intellect, strength, and perseverance live on in her daughter. Iriana is a doctor and the vice president of the Gorbachev Foundation, which works for humanitarian causes around the world.

VALENTINA TERESHKOVA

Colonel-Engineer Valentina Vladimirovna Tereshkova was born in 1937 in Maslennikovo, a small town in western Russia. Like Raisa Gorbacheva and the majority of Russians, Valentina's childhood was marked by poverty and hardship. Her father had been killed in World War II, and her mother was a factory worker struggling to raise three children. At eight years old, Valentina was late in starting school. She would also leave school at the early age of sixteen in order to work in a factory and help support the family. With these early struggles, Valentina may have seemed like an unlikely candidate to become a world-famous Russian hero, but in just a few years, Valentina Tereshkova would become the first woman in space.

Although she had to work to make money, Valentina continued her education by correspondence. She also found time to pursue her passion—skydiving. She joined the local aviation club and then started a parachute club of her own.

At the same time that Valentina was learning to skydive, the Soviet space program was considering a stunt of its own. During the Cold War, the United States and the Soviet Union were not only in a nuclear arms race; they were also in a space race. Seemingly everything in this period was a competition between these two countries: who had better universities, who had better technology, who had the better space program, who had better weapons, and ultimately, which was the better system—Communism and Soviet government, or capitalism and United States' democracy? The Soviet Union had already shown up the United States in two big tests: they had been the first to have a satellite orbit the earth and the first to send a man into space. But now the United States was catching up in the space race, and the Soviet Union needed another first. What,

OUTSTANDING RUSSIAN WOMEN

Russian-born Ayn Rand became a world-famous novelist. Her books are still read around the world.

they wondered, would happen if they became the first country to send a woman into space?

Normally, pilots were chosen to be *cosmonauts*, but this proved a problem for the space program, as there were very few female pilots from which to choose. The Soviet space program extended its search to include parachutists, or skydivers. Among the pilots and parachutists, Valentina and four other women were chosen to enter the rigorous training for space.

Ultimately, only one of these five women would take flight and enter the earth's orbit. All the women completed the strict training, which included physical conditioning, pilot training for jet fighters, spacecraft engineering, and rocket theory. Valentina excelled in some of the areas, but was not the top of the five in every discipline. Nevertheless, she was the one chosen to go into space, and this decision was probably influenced by the fact that Valentina was a strong supporter of the Communist system, a Communist Party member, and displayed none of the "troubling" feminist *ideology* espoused by at least one of the other trainees. For the Soviet leadership, sending a woman into space was, more than anything else, a *propaganda* stunt to bolster its image in the world, so these additional considerations were very important in choosing which woman would enter space.

On June 16, 1963, Valentina Tereshkova took flight on the Vostok 6 and became the first woman in space. Her flight lasted 2.95 days, and in that time her aircraft orbited the earth forty-eight times. After reentry, Valentina was ejected from her space capsule, parachuted back to earth, and landed to find herself an instant celebrity.

In the years directly following her flight, Valentina traveled around the world as a spokesperson for the Soviet government, was a member of the World Peace Council, studied at and graduated with distinction from the Zhukovskii Military Air Academy, married a fellow cosmonaut, and had a daughter. She also received numerous awards and honors including Hero of the Soviet Union,

Order of Lenin, the Joliot-Curie Gold Medal, and the United Nations Gold Medal of Peace.

Despite her success in flight, another Russian woman would not follow in her footsteps until 1982, when Svetlana Savitskaya entered space. Today Valentina Tereshkova lives a quiet life in Moscow.

After Valentina's space flight, a huge controversy ensued as male cosmonauts accused Valentina of poor performance and insubordination during the flight. The claims have never been proven, and some think the male cosmonauts' accusations arose from chauvinism and resentment of Valentina's newfound fame.

"ONE FACES THE FUTURE
WITH ONE'S PAST."
—PEARL BUCK

CHALLENGES FOR THE FUTURE

7

THE ENVIRONMENT

Raisa Gorbacheva once said, "[The natural world's impoverishment] leads to the impoverishment of the human soul. It is related to the outburst of violence in human society. To save the natural world today means to save what is human in humanity."

One of the biggest challenges facing not just women, but all Russian people today is the degradation of their natural environment. Environmentally related health problems ranging from heavy metal poisoning (usually resulting from heavy metals like lead and mercury contaminating the water) to cancer caused by exposure to radiation are common, and if Russia continues on its current path, the risks will only increase in the future.

Many of Russia's environmental problems stem from the Cold War era. For example, during the Cold War, numerous nuclear explosions were detonated underground and continue to radiate today, causing cancer and birth defects in local populations. There were also virtually no environmental regulations on industries, and much of Russia was a dumping ground for toxic waste. In many cases, there aren't even records of where toxic materials were released.

Russian women participate in a demonstration, actively expressing their views.

However, not all Russia's environmental problems can be blamed on the past. Plenty of unsound practices continue today. Though Russia has made strides in some areas of industry regulation, it also has a long way to go. Furthermore, Russia's economic crisis only makes environmental issues worse. It costs a lot of money to clean up past problems and to prevent new ones from emerging. For example, Russia cannot afford to fix its huge oil pipelines, and as a result, the aging system leaks over five million tons of oil a year, creating virtual lakes of toxic material. Similarly, storage facilities for the spent plutonium from Russia's many nuclear reactors need constant monitoring and upkeep to ensure safety. Cutbacks in government funding cause many people to fear the continued safety of stored nuclear materials.

Today, a shocking 15 percent of Russian lands are considered to be ecological disaster areas. In the time just preceding the fall of the Soviet Union, numerous environmental groups were forming, and *grassroots initiatives* were gaining momentum. In recent years, however, the environmental movement in Russia has slowed down. Women are very active in the remaining environmental groups, but with so many struggles simply to survive, many people feel they no longer have time to worry about the environment. However, others realize that if the environment continues to degrade at its present rate, it will become difficult to survive at all.

SEX TRADE AND ORGANIZED CRIME

Another serious challenge facing Russia today is the prevalence of organized crime. Organized crime syndicates have flourished since the fall of Communism. These organizations use violence to gain control of illegal segments of the Russian economy, like the drug and weapons trades. They also make business difficult in all of Russia by demanding things like "protection payments." If you don't make the protection payment, your business may be destroyed, or you may even be killed. Threats from such criminals are extremely intimidating and keep many people, especially women, from attempting to enter business at all.

One branch of organized crime has a particularly damaging effect on women: the sex trade. As a result of poverty, some women have been forced to work as prostitutes, people who have sex in exchange for money or other support. Some women choose to work as prostitutes in Russia, but many others are lured or forced into the trade. Many women are sold into a type of slavery overseas. Criminal gangs use threats and intimidation to gain control over women. Media reports are filled with stories of women and teenage girls being smuggled into Europe. Some of the women who are forced into the sex trade are as young as fifteen. If these women and girls cause any difficulties for the gangsters, threats may be carried out against their families in Russia.

Not all women are intimidated into the sex trade. Other women are tricked into thinking they are getting good jobs like positions as maids or child-care workers. Once the women arrive, however, they realize they've been deceived.

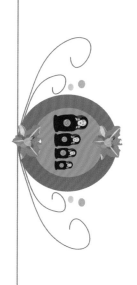

Officials in Russia estimate that 7,500 women have been forced to migrate from Russia to work in the sex trade industry in Europe. Other reports, however, estimate the true number to be 50,000 women each year.

The Russian government is working with the United Nations to protect its children and women.

By this time, however, it is usually too late. They have no money, are being held by dangerous criminals, often don't speak the local language, and have no way of getting home. Attempts are now being made to educate women about these illegal schemes. The Russian parliament has recently begun to work with the United Nations to help prevent the problem. One proposed law would require educating women about the threat of the sex trade, providing services to help rehabilitate the victims of the industry, and forcing officials to work against the problem.

These two examples alone clearly indicate that plenty of challenges face Russia's women—and all of Russia's people. However, challenges are not new

to the Russian people, and today the struggles occur side-by-side with new opportunities and hopes for the future. Russian women today are bolstered by a long history of women who fought for their families, their communities, and themselves. Though born into a patriarchal society, the women of Russia have been proving for thousands of years that they are strong leaders with an indomitable spirit.

FURTHER READING

Baranskaya, Natalya. *A Week Like Any Other: Novellas and Stories.* Seattle, Wash.: Seal Press, 1990.

Berman, Connie. *Anna Kournikova: Women Who Win.* New York: Chelsea House Publishing, 2001.

Carson, Anna R. *Russia.* New York: Chelsea House Publishing, 2002.

Fader, Kim Brown. *Russia.* San Diego, Calif.: Lucent Books, 1998.

Kotlyarskaya, Elena. *Russia: Women in Society.* Tarrytown, N.Y.: Marshall Cavendish, 1994.

Krull, Kathleen. *Lives of Extraordinary Women: Rulers, Rebels (and What the Neighbors Thought).* Orlando, Fla.: Harcourt Inc., 2000.

Millinship, William. *Front Line: Women of the New Russia.* London, U.K.: Methuen London, 1993.

Nickles, Greg. *Russia: The Land.* New York: Crabtree Publishing Company, 2000.

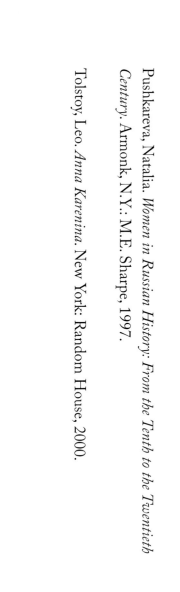

Pushkareva, Natalia. *Women in Russian History: From the Tenth to the Twentieth Century*. Armonk, N.Y.: M.E. Sharpe, 1997.

Tolstoy, Leo. *Anna Karenina*. New York: Random House, 2000.

FOR MORE INFORMATION

Biographies of Notable Women
www.womenshistory.about.com/library/bio/blbio_list.htm

Famous Russian Women
famous.russian-women.net

Initiative for Social Action and Renewal in Eurasia
www.isar.org

Information about Russian people, history, and travel
www.waytorussia.net

Information about Valentina Tereshkova's Space Flight
www.astronautix.com/flights/vostok6.htm

"The Princess who Became Catherine the Great"
www.members.tripod.com/%7ENevermore/CGREAT.HTM

Russian Feminism Resources
www.geocities.com/Athens/2533/activism.html

Russian Women's Microfinance Network Website
www.rwmn.ru/s-d-e.html

The United Nations Website
www.un.org/womenwatch/

The World Factbook
www.cia.gov/cia/publications/factbook/geos/rs.html

Publisher's note:
The Web sites listed on these pages were active at the time of publication. The publisher is not responsible for Web sites that have changed their addresses or discontinued operation since the date of publication. The publisher will review and update the Web sites upon each reprint.

GLOSSARY

amber   A hard yellowish to brownish transparent fossil resin used mainly in making ornamental objects such as beads.

animist   Someone who believes spiritual beings are capable of influencing human events, based on the idea that animals, plants, and even inanimate objects have souls like humans.

aristocracy   Government by a small, privileged ruling class.

atheistic   Having to do with disbelief in God's existence.

boyars   Members of the Russian aristocratic order next in rank to the ruling prince until abolished by Peter the Great.

capitalist system   An economic system characterized by private ownership and a free market.

class hierarchy   Order of social rank.

Common Era   The period dating from the birth of Jesus Christ.

communists   People who believe in a theory that advocates the elimination of private property; communism is a system where goods are owned communally and are made available to all as needed.

correlation   A mutual or reciprocal relation between two things.

cosmonauts   Russian astronauts.

coup   A sudden attempt to overthrow a government.

disempowering   Disenabling; taking away one's authority or power.

economies   Systems concerned with the production, distribution, and consumption of goods and services.

Enlightenment A European philosophical movement of the eighteenth century. Its basic belief was the superiority of reason as a guide to all human concerns and knowledge.

entrepreneurs People who organize, manage, and assume the liabilities of an enterprise or business.

francophones People belonging to a population that uses French as its first or sometimes second language.

genocide The systematic and deliberate destruction of a racial, political, or cultural group.

grassroots initiatives Movements that are organized at the local or lower level of society.

gulag The USSR's penal system consisting of labor camps.

ideology A systematic body of ideas, especially regarding human life or culture.

industrialization The act of becoming socially organized whereby industries, especially large-scale industries, are dominant.

liberal Broad-minded, open to new ideas, progressive.

modernization The act of becoming more up-to-date and contemporary.

Orthodox Having to do with a branch of the Christian church that follows the Byzantine rite of worship.

pariahs Outcasts.

pious Showing reverence for deity and devotion to divine worship.

propaganda The spreading of information, ideas, or rumor for the purpose of helping or harming an institution, cause, or person.

renaissance Rebirth.

serfs Members of a subservient feudal class bound to the land and subject to the will of the lord.

scapegoat Someone who is forced to bear the blame for another person's actions.

stereotypes Things conforming to a fixed pattern, especially mental pictures held by a group that are oversimplified opinions, prejudicial attitudes, or uncritical judgments.

transient Passing through or by a place, staying only briefly.

tribute Excessive tax, rent, or tariff imposed by a government, sovereign, landlord, or lord.

tundra A level or rolling treeless plain, characteristic of arctic and subarctic regions, consisting of black mucky soil with a permanently frozen subsoil, and having a dominant vegetation of lichens, herbs, mosses, and dwarf shrubs.

INDEX

PICTURE CREDITS

Artville: p. 6

Michelle Bouch: pp. 10, 14, 16, 19, 20, 23, 25, 26, 29, 32, 49, 52, 66, 76, 86, 88, 90, 93, 96

Corel: pp. 12, 30, 38, 40, 42, 45 46, 47, 50, 54, 57, 58, 63, 64, 68, 71, 72

Viola Ruelke Gommer: pp. 34, 60, 74, 81, 82, 101

Eric Schwartz: pp. 79, 98

BIOGRAPHIES

Autumn Libal is a freelance author and illustrator living in Vancouver, British Columbia. She received her degree from Smith College, an all women's college in Northampton, Massachusetts, where she developed a deep interest in women's issues. Autumn's writing has also appeared in *New Moon: The Magazine for Girls and Their Dreams*, as well as other Mason Crest series including, NORTH AMERICAN FOLKLORE and NORTH AMERICAN INDIANS TODAY.

Dr. Mary Jo Dudley is the director of Cornell University's Gender and Global Change Department, which focuses on the evolving role of gender around the world. She is also the associate director of Latin American Studies at Cornell.